A. Lincoln.

LINCOLN
AS THE SOUTH
SHOULD KNOW HIM

by
Oscar William Blacknall

THE CONFEDERATE
REPRINT COMPANY
☆   ☆   ☆   ☆
WWW.CONFEDERATEREPRINT.COM

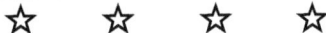

Lincoln as the South Should Know Him
by Oscar William Blacknall

Originally Published in 1915
Manly's Battery Chapter, Children of the Confederacy
Raleigh, North Carolina

Reprint Edition © 2016
The Confederate Reprint Company
Post Office Box 2027
Toccoa, Georgia 30577
www.confederatereprint.com

Cover and Interior Design by
Magnolia Graphic Design
www.magnoliagraphicdesign.com

ISBN-13: 978-1945848056
ISBN-10: 1945848057

In a blaze of burning roof-trees,
    under clouds of smoke and flame,
Sprang a new word into being,
    from a stern and dreaded name;
Gaunt and grim and like a specter
    rose that word before the world,
From a land of bloom and beauty
    into ruin rudely hurled.
From a people scourged by exile,
    from a city ostracized,
Pallas-like it sprang to being –
    and that word is "Shermanized."

L. Virginia French.

CHAPTER ONE

☆ ☆ ☆ ☆

What thick hides and short memories we Southern folk have, and how inconsistent we are! We call down anathema on the Kaiser's head for the devastation of Belgium; in almost the same breath we raise pæans to Lincoln, who was responsible for the far more causeless and ruthless devastation of the South by Sherman – Sherman, who waged war so atrocious that its very author could find no name on earth to match, but had to go down below to get it. Well might he, with Milton's Satan, say

"Where I am is hell."

Satan lit its fires in his own breast; Sherman, in the desolated homes of war, made widows and orphans.

If Belgium had its Louvain and Antwerp, so also had the South its Columbia, its Atlanta, its Savannah, its Charleston.

Countless Belgium homes have been burned. But there has been nothing like systematic, utter destruction. The Kaiser, outnumbered, hard beset, the very existence of his country in imminent peril has increased his slender stoic of food by robbing Belgium, electing to starve foe rather than friend. (This was written in January, 1915.) That vengeance, not necessity, prompted the black path that Sherman cut through the South, the evidence is full and damning. On December 18, 1864, General Halleck, Chief of Staff to President Lincoln, and necessarily in close touch with him, writes to Sherman as follows: "Should you capture Charleston, I hope by some accident the place will be destroyed. And if a little salt can be sown on its site, it may prevent the future growth of nullification and secession."

Sherman, on the 24th, answers as follows: "I will bear in mind your hint as to Charleston, and do not think that 'salt' will be necessary. When I move, the Fifteenth Corps will be on the right of the right wing, and their position will naturally bring them into Charleston first; and if you have watched the history of that corps you will have remarked that they do their work pretty well. The truth is, the whole army is burning with an insatiable desire to wreak vengeance on South Carolina."

One of Wheeler's scouts, observing Sherman's advance, reported that during one night, and from one point, he counted over one hundred burning homes. And as to the looting, a letter written by a Federal officer, and found at Camden, S.C., after the army passed, and given in the *Southern Woman's Magazine*, runs as follows: "We have had a glorious time in this State. The chivalry have been stripped of most of their valuables. Gold watches, silver pitchers, cups, spoons, forks, etc., are as common in camp as blackberries. Of rings, earrings, and breastpins I have a quart. I am not joking – I have at least a quart of jewelry for you and the girls, and some No. 1 diamond pins and rings among them. Don't show this letter out of the family."

Sherman long denied burning Columbia, in the most solemn manner calling his God to witness as to his truthfulness. When, after the overwhelming evidence that he did burn it was adduced, he unblushingly admitted the fact, and that he had lied on Wade Hampton with the purpose of rendering him unpopular, and thereby weakening his cause. But a mere lie shines white against the black ground of Sherman's character.

I could pile up a mountain of facts as damning as those given. But what boots it to prove again what too long ago has been proven – that not since Attila, "The Scourge of God," cut his black swath across Europe fifteen hundred years ago has Sherman's "March to the Sea" had its fellow.

The conversion of the Shenandoah region into a waste so complete that, in Sheridan's own words, a crow flying over it would have had to carry his rations – a destruction not only of every vestige of food, of all animals and fowls, but also of every implement that could be used to make or prepare more food, every millstone, wagon, plow, rake, and harrow, down to the flower-hoes of the women, may have been a military necessity, for this lovely valley was, in some measure, the granary of Lee's army.

The necessities of war demanded that Sherman live off the country he traversed. Those elastic necessities may have been stretched to demand that he destroy even the pitiful stint of food that the South had left; that he wrest the last morsel from the mouth of the mother and babe, lest, perchance, some crumb thereof reach and nourish the men at the front. But what necessity of war, except that brand that Sherman fathered and sponsored, demanded that the torch follow the pillager, that every home be burned, and famishing mother and babe be turned out in midwinter to die of cold and exposure?

"But didn't 'Sherman's March' shorten the war; didn't it shake Lee's lines around Petersburg when his men knew that fire and rapine were in their homes?" is sometimes asked. Doubtless. And it might have shaken them all the more had wives and babes been burnt in these homes rather than left to starve in their ruins. It might have been not only more effective but more merciful. But there are abysmal depths of atrocity from which even the "hired assassin" recoils – that is, unless he belongs to the Attilas, Alvas, and Shermans. There are rules of civilized warfare which the soldier in every extremity must observe or else have heaped upon him the execration of mankind.

The whole world shudders at the robbery and partial ruin of only a part of Belgium. Sherman devastated an area nearly twice as great is the whole of Belgium and devastated it utterly, leaving only blackened chimneys and starving women and children in his wake. That his hell was only some sixty miles wide was owing to no lack of Satanic ferocity on his part. It would have been much wider had not Wheeler, with his handful of horse, hung close to Sherman's flanks, with a quick halter for every marauder he caught in the act. Sherman's little finger was heavier than the whole martial first of the Kaiser. Belgium was a battle-ground – the largest and fiercest that even blood-soaked old Mother Earth ever saw. But it took five million men five months to work wreck and ruin; Sherman did it overnight night with sixty thousand. The Kaiser found at least a potential sniper in every window; his every step was a battle. Sherman had only a light screen of cavalry to brush aside, and not always even that.

That there was less starvation in Sherman's path than the Kaiser's – though many a high-born Southern lady kept life in her children for the time with the waste corn slobbered from the mouths of the Federal cavalry and artillery horses – was because the South was large and far less densely populated than Belgium, and that the victims sought shelter in the unravaged regions which Wheeler had saved.

Then there is a hideous chapter in this black book that never has and never will be written – so hideous that even the South has been fain to draw over it the curtain of oblivion. I mean the violence that Southern women suffered at the hands of Sherman's ruffians. It is a well-known fact, and by none better known than by military men themselves, that men herded in camps, removed from the restraints of home, rapidly tend to relapse towards barbarism, and that only the iron hand of discipline can hold them in check. Relax that discipline in one respect, sanction the perpetration of one crime, and all crimes, especially the crime against woman, follows as a natural sequence.

No one who lived in or near Sherman's path in Georgia, South Carolina, or even in this State, after the war was over and the troops marching for disbandment in Washington, can lack knowledge of cases that came to light, despite every effort of the hapless victims themselves to hide them. To recall only the cases which abide with me most vividly, that came practically under my own observation, or that I had first-hand knowledge of – the beautiful girl to whose rescue came one of Wheeler's troopers, and who, seized and used as a shield by the ruffian who had abused her, in her agony begged the trooper to shoot through her body and kill him; but by a dexterous movement the brute was killed over her shoulder.

The cottage, with its rose-covered porch, in which lived the young widow and her three daughters, all noted for their beauty and refinement, at whose door a hand of Federal troopers drew rein at dusk – the screams and sobs that all the live-long night the neighbors heard, but dared not stir – the tomblike aspect of the cottage, with no smoke from the chimneys, no sign of life, for days and days afterwards – the deep grave of forgetfulness that the sorrowing neighborhood dug for the whole horrible affair, where it rests this day. The very first offense of a Negro against a white woman that I ever heard of was committed in this neighborhood, in April, 1865, by one who had been under Sherman's tutelage. What, indeed, was the saturnalia of crime against Southern woman for a generation afterwards but the aftermath, the legacy, of that foulest blot on American history – Sherman's vaunted "March to the Sea"?

CHAPTER TWO

☆ ☆ ☆ ☆

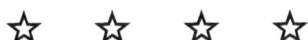

It is a maxim of war, as it is of common sense, that the higher the rank the greater the fame or blame for any given act. In every crime that sprang from this lack of discipline – and no one can question that practically all did so spring – the men higher up, who invited the crime by lowering the bars of discipline, were worse criminals than the perpetrators themselves. Above the perpetrator stood the commander of the army, Sherman; above Sherman stood the commander-in-chief of all the Federal armies, Abraham Lincoln. If Lincoln ever discountenanced Sherman and his methods, he never gave voice to it, and he was a man of many words.

George III., whom we were reared to execrate next to Satan, and Lincoln, whom our children are being reared to venerate almost next to God, both sent armies to invade the South – the one in the benighted eighteenth, the other in the enlightened nineteenth century. Surely the character and conduct of the two commanders put at the head of these invading armies must be some indication of the animus of those two men towards the South. I quote first from Cornwallis's order book, various late of January, February, and March, 1781, showing him to have been more careful to shield noncombatants from the pettiest theft than Sherman was to save them from the blackest crimes:

"It is needless to point out to officers the necessity of preserving the strictest discipline and of preventing the oppressed people from suffering by the hands of those from whom they are taught to look for protection. Lord Cornwallis is highly displeased that several houses have been set on fire today during the march – a disgrace to the army – and he will punish with the utmost severity any person or persons found guilty of committing so disgraceful an outrage. His lordship requests that the commanding officers of the corps will endeavor to find the persons who set fire to the houses this day."

"Great complaints have been made of negroes straggling, plundering, and using violence. No negroes shall be suffered to carry arms. Provost marshal has orders to shoot on the spot any negro who may offend against these regulations."

"Any officer who looks on and does not do his utmost to prevent shameful marauding will be considered in a more criminal light than the person who committed these scandalous crimes."

"A woman having been robbed of a watch, a black silk handkerchief, a gallon of peach brandy, and a shirt, and, by the description, by a soldier of the Guard, every man's kit is to be immediately examined."

"All foraging parties will give receipts for the supplies taken by them."

In one instance two staff officers were actually captured because they had remained behind to pay for supplies requisitioned for the invading army.

"A watch found by the regiment of Bose. The owner may have same from adjutant on proving property."

"Immediate inspection of the clothing in possession of the women is to be made. Their clothing to be regularly examined at proper intervals hereafter, and every article found in addition thereto burned at the head of the company. Officers are ordered to make the examination at such tunes as to prevent the women [supposed to be the source of this infamous plundering] from evading the purport of the order."

(Sherman's majors general brought their harlots along, loaded them with stolen jewelry, and desecrated Southern homes with them overnight before applying the torch next morning.)

I might quote at great length the British commander's restraining words and cite instances of stronger measures, but will cite only one.

After Cornwallis's virtual defeat at Guilford he retreated to Wilmington, then passed northward through the State on the way to his doom at Yorktown. Even if policy rather than principle had influenced him earlier in the campaign, it could have had little weight with him then, for, as he well knew, the game was lost. While at Halifax tidings reached him that a woman had suffered at the hands of Tarleton's troopers forming his advance guard. Taking a body-guard of only one dragoon, Cornwallis spurred forward and overtook Tarleton near the present town of Garysburg. The whole command was halted till witnesses could be brought up. It was then dismounted, lined up, the two offenders, one a sergeant, identified, tried by drumhead court-martial, and strung up to the nearest tree.

So much for the army that the tyrant, George III., sent. Eighty-four years later the superman, Lincoln, sent an army along much the same track. The object of both armies was to subdue the invaded region and win it back to their respective governments.

The tyrant of the eighteenth century, as we have seen, sought to subdue by waging honorable warfare against combatants and protecting the person and property of noncombatants.

And the superman? To devastate and utterly ruin every inch of territory that the far-flung wings of his great army could compass – a compass limited only by the activity of the Confederate cavalry on its flanks.

Even then, if in the conflict of the strong North against the weak South such cruel measures were necessary, if the occasion demanded that every Southern woman and child that could be reached be deprived of food, clothing, and shelter, and turned out in midwinter, it does seem that this superman would have sent the sanest and humanest of all his lieutenants to accomplish this fell work – would have tempered wrath with mercy. Instead, he sent Sherman, the demoniac. Charity impels me to dub him only demoniac, possessed of a demon, rather than to believe one of my own species could be demon outright. Listen at his ravings and judge. They are taken at random from his orders and reports, and whole pages could be filled with such venomous utterances:

"As to the Kentucky secessionists, I hope General Burbridge will send them to Dry Tortugas [a sandy island of insufferable heat and glare south of Florida] – men, women, and children – and encourage a new breed."

"Hang a few secessionists now and then."

"I am going into the very bowels of the Confederacy, and propose to leave a trail that will be recognized for fifty years."

"I propose to sally forth to ruin Georgia, and expect to leave a hole that will be hard to mend."

"I am perfecting arrangements to push into Georgia and make desolation everywhere. I will make Georgia howl."

"Arrest all people, male and female, and let them foot it into Marietta. Let them take their children and clothing, provided they have means of hauling them." (Lacking these means, the only inference is that both were to be left behind.)

"I propose to march, leaving a patch of desolation behind."

"I will see that Atlanta is utterly ruined."

And like master like man. Small wonder that Sherman's underlings filled every item down the long, black list of crime, from plain stealing to arson, rape, and murder. Lack of space forbids that I even classify the fiendishness – from the midnight burning of towns, driving the unprotected women and girls into the streets crowded with unrestrained soldiery, to slipping the quid of tobacco into the pitiful jug of sorghum, which the mother, everything else destroyed, had saved from her blazing home and held desperately to as the last bar between her little brood and actual starvation; the spattering of the little tot with blood as the calf was shot in her arms, she having hugged it tight to save it from the fate of horses, cows, sheep, pigs, and poultry shot down and left to rot around the house.

Decency bars me from more than hinting at the wanton and studied befoulment of precious heirlooms and sacred things before applying the torch, and all the insults and outrages that helpless woman has to endure from brutal man when the clock is set back to primeval savagery. It is all-sufficing to say that as a rule they did their level best to match with their own black deeds their leader's black words. It would take a pen with the three-league sweep of Kipling's artist's brush in the hereafter to do justice to the breadth and depth of it all – and then no mind could comprehend it all and retain its saneness.

Sherman apologists (I never heard of his having a defender) have cited the liberal terms he offered Johnston and his remonstrance with the

Northern politicians as to their treatment of the South after the war as showing that he was not all black. As to the terms offered Johnston, I would say that that was all a matter of policy in which motives of humanity might and might not have had a part. As to the other, judging the man by his deeds and knowing his animus towards the politician, I am forced to suspect that his motives were akin to those that prompted Macaulay's Puritan to condemn bear-baiting – not that it gave pain to bear, but that it gave pleasure to man. Or was it, rather, that, like the hyena, having mangled his helpless prey, he was jealous of the jackal pack?

CHAPTER THREE

☆ ☆ ☆ ☆

That Lincoln was an able man, of many
amiable qualities, is wholly beside the point. The
colossal public crimes of history were committed
by men altogether amiable, or estimable, or both,
in private life. Julius Cæsar, the destroyer of
ancient liberty, was the most genial and compan-
ionable of men. Charles the First, who but for the
headsman might have destroyed modern liberty,
was a tender-hearted, lovable gentleman of stain-
less private life, as was Robespierre, who glutted
the very guillotine with innocent blood. Who
could out-cajole Napoleon or Louis the Four-
teenth, arch enemies of mankind, or, as to that,
Satan himself? Did it brighten the lot of the shell-
torn inmates of Southern hospitals to know that
the maker of medical and surgical supplies, contraband of war, was a man of infinite jest? Were
the skeletons rotting in the vermin-encrusted bur-

rows of Andersonville, or freezing in the icy sheds of Point Lookout and Fort Delaware, helped by knowing that the breaker of the cartel could not abide the sight of misery? Did it lessen the sorrow of Southern mothers, who, roof-trees ablaze, fled with their little broods to the wintry woods and swamps, to know that the hand that swayed the bosom of hell always rested tenderly on the head of his own children? Did it diminish the agony of Southern maidens, writhing in the clutches of Sherman's licentious soldiery, to remember that the one at the head of it all was a virtuous man?

Lincoln, the public man – the only Lincoln that we knew – was the creature of the Republican Party – the party born of anti-Southernism, anti-Jeffersonism, the innate and truceless foe of individual, local liberty, as opposed to centralism, imperialism.

Did Lincoln ever rise a hair's breadth above his party? Is there a single instance in which he failed to see with its eyes, act with its spirit? When, during the opening, progress, or close of the war, did he display that greatness of mind or of heart, that magnanimity, that should wrest homage from even a vanquished and ruined foe? When or where was he other than the incarnation of Republicanism?

Shall we honor him for the dexterity, not to say duplicity, with which the Peace Commissioners, the able men whom the South sent to Washington in March, 1861, in a strenuous endeavor to avert war, were kept dangling, while in violence to solemn promise the secret expedition was prepared and despatched to reinforce Sumter, a measure so close akin to perfidy that it alarmed and enraged the South and precipitated war?

It has been a platitude of history that the war was inevitable. Like most platitudes, it has very little thought back of it. In exact proportion as we disentangle the skein of past diplomacy and past politics, in the same degree do we discern that few if any wars were inevitable. In public no less than in private life the soft answer turneth away wrath. At one touch of a frank, honest, sympathetic hand the most sinister political kaleidoscopes in history have instantly assumed benign combinations.

But that is all by the way. The wisest men of that day did not think war inevitable. Men North and South were working hard for peace. Lincoln's words and actions made only for war. How different was Washington's action in Shay's rebellion! Not waiting for overtures, he took the initiative and appointed a commission to confer with the malcontents, and thus averted bloodshed.

Shall we honor Lincoln for his Emancipation Proclamation? The blackest crime laid at the door of George III. was that he unleashed a handful of savages against our frontiers. Lincoln, as far as in him lay, unleashed four million savages (which the North held that slavery had converted the Negro into) in our very midst, against our defenseless women and children. To the good feelings existing between the races we chiefly owe that the horrors of St. Domingo, multiplied ten thousandfold, were not repeated at the South.

Shall we honor him for the flagrant breach of the cartel, and the resulting hells – Point Lookout, Fort Delaware, Johnson Island, Camp Morton, Camp Chase, Rock Island, at the North; Andersonville, Belle Isle, Salisbury at the South, and many more prisons in each Republic?

Shall we honor him for out-Kaisering the Kaiser in making medical and surgical supplies contraband of war, thus adding still lower depths to those hells, as to the whole war, on the Southern side?

Shall we honor him for Sherman's Gargantuan orgy of crime in Georgia and South Carolina, and for the vile dregs of it that our own women had to drain long after the hostilities ceased?

Lincoln's tragic taking off naturally caused

a great revulsion of feeling in his favor at the South. This has prompted us to believe that had he lived the Republican lion would have transfigured itself into a lamb the moment that

> "The war drums ceased from throbbing
> And the battle flags were furled."

In other words, that mildness and benignancy quite angelic would have marked the reconstruction period, or rather there would have been no reconstruction period at all, but, instead, a kind of family reunion, with Seward, Ben Wade, and Thad Stevens *et id* as ecstatic ushers.

But from what act of Lincoln's do we find justification for this belief, or rather hope? There were good words enow. For, statesman as he was, Lincoln was first, last, and always the politician, seeking the public will before the public weal. Not by words, but deeds, must a man be judged. Words are the politician's stock in trade. "Deeds proclaim the man"; words too often hide him. It is true that when Richmond fell he authorized the calling together of the Virginia Legislature. But it was avowedly because he believed that it would recall the Virginia troops from Lee's retreating army, and he wished to give opportunity to do so. The moment that Lee surrendered he withdrew the permit, and ordered the arrest of any members

members who disobeyed the order to quit Richmond promptly.

It is far more likely than otherwise that Lincoln's death lightened the heel that sought to grind us in the mire. The incarnation of Republicanism in war, there is not a shadow of reason for believing that in peace he could have thwarted the politicians of their prey, though he would no doubt have deprecated their violence.

Why, pray, should he who shut his eyes while 18,000 square miles of Southern homes were being Shermanized, converted into a hell more vast and hideous than even Milton's imagination ever winged, all under plea of military necessity, have been less pliant when, a little later, political necessity called? Are Southern institutions more sacred than Southern women? Does the South set a greater value upon her political welfare than on the lives of her children, and the honor of her women?

The Republican politicians were bent upon the utter humiliation and degradation of the South; upon forcing on her civil rights, miscegenation, and mongrelism. Their animus is shown by the clash with Andy Johnson, the fierce fight against even the stint of justice that a renegade would fain have accorded the land of his birth. So fraught was their attitude to the South with malice prepense that they in a measure overreached themselves, and brought about a partial reaction of feeling among the Northern people at large. Then the scrimmage with Johnson distracted their attention. He got many a blow that would otherwise have fallen on our defenseless head. Under Lincoln, their methods would almost surely have been less violent, but probably far more systematic and insidious. Davis might not have been imprisoned, or not so long, or Wirz, the commandant of Andersonville prison, executed. But in all likelihood a more furtive, deadly way would have been found to work our undoing. When thieves fall out honest men thrive, and that is about the only chance they do get to thrive.

The man to whom is really due the gratitude of the South is Grant. Had he not scotched the plan of the Republicans to punish the Southern military leaders, by threatening to throw up his commission if Lee was arrested, there is no telling, the gates of vengeance once ajar, when they would ever have closed.

Turning from Lincoln the Republican to Lincoln the man – Is the wily, not to say tricky, politician, the reveler in "smutty" jokes, the Southern ideal? Lack we, of our own kith and kind, of our own household of faith, great men who were also great gentlemen? Are we so poor in heroes that we must needs pedestal the man who led his section somewhat bunglingly, it is true, but without ruth or remorse in the onslaught that virtually destroyed ours?

Again, is there anything in the achievement of Lincoln so dazzling that it should blind us to everything else? Is there glory for the strong in overcoming the weak; the many the few? Would we ever have heard of Goliath, Xerxes, Darius, and all their like, had they won? Such immortality that they won is reflected from the foes they faced, weaker but of better mettle.

CHAPTER FOUR

☆ ☆ ☆ ☆

In years to come the case of the South and the North will be cited as the crowning instance of the tyranny of the pen. The American colonies, equal sisters, finding themselves aggrieved by certain unmotherly measures of the mother country – a mother too far off to harm them greatly, and in fact harming only their pocket, and that slightly, yet made war on her, the author of their being, beat her and set up for themselves, calling high heaven to witness that "Governments derive their just powers from the consent of the governed."

Now, some malign power had laid upon all, or about all, of these sister colonies a great burden, a great curse (negro slavery), disguised as a blessing, but upon part of them more heavily than others. The sisters lightly afflicted were able to free themselves of this curse not only without scathe, but with actual profit, by shifting their portion of it upon those sisters sorely afflicted to helplessness.

Then straightway the free sisters, seeing how trammeled and helpless the burdened sisters were, not only robbed their pockets by iniquitous tariff laws which bore heaviest on one section, but, what was infinitely worse, they turned their quacks (the Abolitionists) loose on them with their nostrums, defeating all the practical efforts of the burdened sisters to cure themselves. Finally, forced thereto by the instinct of self-preservation, the first law of nature, the burdened sisters, now expanded into a domain larger than the whole at the beginning, and three times as populous, took steps to save themselves, to be rid of the persecuting sisters. But these steps were far more deliberate, more orderly, and far more conciliatory than those taken with the mother country at the Revolution.

With all solemnity, observing every form of law and diplomacy, they declared their independence by withdrawing from the Union, as the persecuting sisters had, under infinitely less provocation, repeatedly threatened to do; and, when driven to the wall, turned and defended this "inalienable right," that "Governments derive their just powers from the consent of the governed," with a courage and devotion that never has been surpassed.

That their appeal to the sword should have been lost is no wonder. The sword has ever been the slave of might.

But that a people who so long withstood the sword of the North should have surrendered so quickly, so cravenly, to its pen, must forever stand the wonder of the world. It will be incredible that an intelligent, high-spirited people, a people showing in every other respect mental and moral fiber of the most robust order, should have been transfigured into such groveling thralls that they not only forswore the high, expressive, and honorable name of the struggle given by their fathers, "The War for Southern Independence," but came to see only wild political folly, madness, in the sane and heroic endeavors of the fathers to establish and maintain a republic suited to the genius of the Southern people, one in which issues the most portentous that ever faced any people could have been settled by these people themselves and not by the arbitrary and hostile power of an alien people, or rather left unsettled, and in such a posture that, like Banquo's ghost, it would never down.

The compromise name, "War Between the States," which our perhaps overcautious leaders thought best to use while the South still had her head in the lion's mouth, was, as they must have known, a clear misnomer. But a misnomer, a wrong name, they doubtless held, was better than a bad one, better than the name rebellion with all its load of opprobrium and reproach.

Nevertheless, whatever the war was, it was not a war between the States. The States, as States, took no part in it, were not even known in it. It was a war between two thoroughly organized governments and for one great principle, that completely overshadowed all others – Southern Independence. To the Northern mind the struggle of the South to reassert the cardinal principle of the Declaration of Independence, that all men are entitled to life, liberty, and the pursuit of happiness, was rebellion; to the Southern mind it was not.

To every patriotic Southerner, War for Southern Independence should be a sacred name. It is the name hallowed by the lips of the men who died to make it a reality.

To all of us, from Jeff. Davis and Zeb. Vance down to the smallest "shaver" who waved his home-made straw hat to a frazzle as the soldier trains rolled by, it was the "War for Southern Independence"; never a war between the States. To the thousands who died that the name might live, who breathed out their gallant lives amid the smoke and dead-fallen air of battle, or who, braver still, starving in Northern prisons, surrendered to the fell Sergeant Death rather than to the wiles of the captor who offered the renegade everything, it was always, everywhere, the War for Southern Independence. They never believed they were dying in a mere squabble between States, but to achieve Southern Independence; to erect a great Southern Republic, under whose golden ægis Southern civilization would flower into the glory and envy of the whole world.

It is treason, rank treason, to their memory for us to dub it otherwise.

CHAPTER FIVE

☆　☆　☆　☆

"What is History But a Lie Agreed Upon?"
– Napoleon.

In the first edition of the foregoing part of this brochure I endeavored to reach the Southern people through my usual channel, the Southern press. To my very great astonishment I found it closed to me. Editors who for nearly forty years had met me more than half way for copy (my pen, since as a young man I gave up a remunerative career as a magazine writer, has been devoted to the defense of the ideals and aspirations of the Old South) now slammed the door in my face. Thus was I driven to appeal to Cæsar, to appeal in pamphlet form from the Southern press to the Southern people.

Their response has been most cordial, showing that whatever the Southern press may be, the Southern people themselves are patriotic.

But men and women pass; the printed word endures. What the papers are today the people must be tomorrow or the day after.

"But for Lincoln's influence you might not here and now dare to write as freely as you do" is the gist of some of the editorial criticism my paper has met, though it was a layman who expressed it in those words.

I submit that it is high time that the patriotic men and women of this generation register a most emphatic protest against the attitude of a part of the press and people before it is too late.

Did we need just what we got in the sixties, and ought we to be shouting glad we got it?

Shades of the Fathers! We, of the purest strain of the stock that gave freedom to the world; we, from whose very loins sprang the architect, the builder and the defender of American liberty – we, so poor in statecraft, so bankrupt in morality, that an alien must needs come with three million at his back, and with fire, sword, and rapine save us from ourselves! Yet such is the logical, the inescapable deduction from the premises our children will be taught to accept!

The North, flinging to us the dross of physical prowess and purblind devotion to a fallacious cause, has arrogated to herself the gold of moral rectitude and political infallibility. We have been taught, and are tamely accepting the dictum that the South, when she lost hold on the motherly apron strings, when she foolishly ventured from under the ægis of Northern protection, relapsed swiftly towards despotism and anarchy, and that Appomattox alone saved us from political disintegration!

Is this true? Do we alone deserve the odium of being the one branch of the race too weak to frame civil institutions that could stand the crucible of war? The Romans, the sanest and most practical political people the world has ever seen, always when the ship of state was in peril, put a dictator at the helm.

"Inter Anna Leges Silent."

In the clash of arms, law was silent, suspended. Private right, private wrong, had to wait until the foe was vanquished and Rome safe.

Rome, when beset the hardest, never faced the disadvantages, and was rarely ever in the extremity that the Confederacy stood from beginning to end. Never in any land was there direr need that a hand, strong, arbitrary, untrammeled by peace-built law and usage, garnering every man, every resource, should strike as one at the Giant Foe.

Yet was there a dictatorship at the South,

or any semblance of one? Did war submerge law? It is a maxim of our race – Free speech, free press, free land. Tyranny ever chains first the tongue, strikes her first blow at the palladium of liberty – free utterance.

Right here in North Carolina the Confederate Government had its fullest swing. The State lay nearer to Richmond (and distance, owing to crude transportation facilities, was a far more formidable thing then than now) than any other State was largely free from invasion. It affords a fair instance of the contact of the Confederate Government with the civil life of the people.

Now, living evidence is still abundant that no man was molested for opinion's sake or for word spoken. That the press remained unmuzzled, the files of the *Raleigh Standard*, which to the very end preached stark treason to the Confederacy, stands in everlasting evidence.

Governor Vance of North Carolina and Governor Brown of Georgia, though patriotic men, seeing fit, even in extremity, to place State rights and other considerations before Confederate success, hampered the Confederate executive to a degree never before or since tolerated under such circumstances. It is true that the impressment and conscription measures were grievous burdens, especially here in such close reach; but they were laws of the Congress, and not the fiat of the Executive. In short, much of the defensive power of the South was lost by the failure of President Davis to wield the full measure of power that would readily have been acquiesced in by the people at large. Never, not even in the greatest crises, did Jefferson Davis exercise one-tenth the dominance over the Confederate Congress that Woodrow Wilson now does over the Federal. Davis's decrease of popularity towards the end came from no abuse of power on his part, but mainly from the stigma which the world attaches to failure – that is, except in case of the soldier. Around him war flings a saving halo.

Let us glance at the other side of the picture – at the status of the civilian of the North. The Federal Government, infinitely superior in resources, had not the same urgent need for unity. Yet we find its actions immeasurably more arbitrary than those of the Confederate Government. Not under the old regime in France were *lettres de cachet* as plentiful or more potent. It was a well-known boast of Stanton, Secretary of War, that he could touch a bell on his table and order the instant arrest of any man in the Union.[1] Fort McHenry at Baltimore, Fort LaFayette at New

---

1. It was actually William H. Seward, Lincoln's Secretary of State, who thus boasted.

York, Fort Warren in Boston Harbor, and the old Capitol Prison at Washington, became veritable bastiles, crammed with political prisoners, men immured for what they had said or for what it was suspected they might say or do. In the old Capitol Prison, at least, executions were frequent.

CHAPTER SIX

☆ ☆ ☆ ☆

Never imposed Fate a heavier burden on any people than on the South when she was made the ladder on which the benighted African must climb to civilization and Christianity. Not the opprobrium, but the profound sympathy of the whole world, and especially of the Negro himself, is our just due; for never, since time began, has a race climbed from darkness to light so swiftly and at so small a price to itself – at such fearful cost to the instrument of its elevation.

As is well known, slavery was no Southern indigene; no plant that grew here only. It was only the inheritance of the ages. Sanctioned by immemorial and universal usage, and even by Holy Writ itself, it was indeed the very oldest of all human institutions. Founded originally, in part at least, upon morality, upon the pity which spared instead of slaying the captive, it thus became the bedrock of all civilization. But slavery in this land, and at that date, was a thing strangely out of place and out of time. So much so, indeed, that one wonders as to Fate's motive in the misplacement. Did a spirit of impish irony impel her, or was she actuated by a deeper motive, when she dropped this Old World estray, this foundling in the cradle of liberty, the New World – the motive that as we "broadened with the act of Freedom," we should also "grow strong beneath the weight of duty"?

Slavery would surely have gone, even had Lincoln never been born. The drift of the world had set against it, deep and resistless. Harking back two thousand years to Epictetus, it had come to see that not to him who getteth, but to him who doeth a wrong, cometh the chief harm. Emancipation was inevitable, and to hold that the Southern people, the purest-blooded branch of the sane and virile Anglo-Saxon race – the race which gave liberty to the world, and which in all lands and under all conditions had stood for justice and fair play, as it came to see it – for us to hold that this, our branch, would have been so degenerate, so recreant to the genius and spirit of the stock, so inferior to its forbears, or even to the "lesser breeds" to the south of us that did put it by, that it lacked the manhood to free itself from the incubus of slavery, is a worse slander than even our foes would dare put upon us.

It is argued, and by our own writers as well as others, that the slave-holding class dominated the South, and that self-interest, cupidity, would always have impelled this class to block emancipation. I would reply that slavery in divers forms was long an institution with our race; but that the race in its progress put it by, despite the strenuous opposition of the slave-holding class – as it must have done in this case. The whole moral trend of the race rendered any other course impossible. The fact that medieval serf was white and strong, and the modern slave black and weak, would undoubtedly have made the work of emancipation harder; but the race is morally stronger now than then.

There is one fact generally overlooked, which would have added greatly to the practicability of emancipation. That was the fact that the slave-holding classes at the South were in a minority of about six to one. Every reform, social or political, that our race has achieved has been in the face of a wealthy minority far stronger than that. In fact, it is almost a truism of our politics that the people, as opposed to aristocracy, always win in the long run. No civilization has survived in which the rule did not hold. The chief reason that the dust covers so many of the splendid civilizations of the past was because the great mass of the people remained inert to the end. The broadening of the franchise right here in North Carolina in the fifties, whereby the aristocratic dominance of the State Senate was abolished, is significant proof of what the middle-class manhood of that generation were capable of.

One thing is certain: Had the Negro remained in our midst the South would have avoided the irretrievable error of the North in making the slave a citizen first and a man afterwards. As emancipation would have been gradual, so also would have been the elevation of the freedmen. As he attained the full stature of manhood, so he must perforce have been invested with the rights and privileges of a man. But he hardly would have remained. Colonization being impracticable at that late period, segregation would probably have been the solution of the race problem. Even in this sanctimonious age we exclude the Asiatic. Where would have been the sin in settling the African in a prescribed area of the country, and excluding him from the other parts of it? Compared with the Yellow peril, the Black peril is Olympus to a wart.

Some degrees of wrong and injustice there might have been. Wrong and injustice are not often absent from the affairs of this world. But who is bold enough to assert that the measure of them could have equaled, or even distantly approached, that infinitude of injustice and of wrong – that orgy of political madness – reconstruction, whose blighting effect was to distract and stunt, perhaps forever, the development of the Negro, and to sow, as far as the hand of malice could sow, the very salt of annihilation over the civilization and life of the South?

As is well known, the emancipation movement in its earlier, saner stages had its warmest and ablest supporters at the South. Washington, Jefferson, Henry, Madison, and the foremost men of that time sought earnestly for some practicable method of putting an end to slavery, which was generally regarded as a curse, and especially so to the whites. But for the perfectly natural reaction caused by the rabid, incendiary methods of the Abolitionists, which, beginning about 1830, flowered so quickly and hideously in the Nat Turner butchery of white women and children, gradual emancipation would soon have been under way, and would almost surely have ended slavery with that century. I would not deny that the development of cotton growing caused by the perfection of the cotton gin, and the resulting enormous increase in slave values, would have made emancipation a tremendous problem. But sphinxes – political, social, industrial, moral, religious, racial – had lined the pathway of our race down the ages. All had been answered, and, we believe, answered right, by the communities which had most at stake.

To our branch alone was denied the price-less boon of answering for themselves the most momentous problem of them all – a problem that involves not only our prosperity, but our very existence, and which now can only deepen and darken with the passage of the centuries. Were our immediate forbears – the men whose courage and heroism in war placed the Lost Cause in fame's eternal keeping, whose fortitude and sa-gacity triumphed even over reconstruction, who hurled back the envenomed dart, Negro suffrage, upon the heads that sent it – weaklings, men whose destiny was safer in the hands of an alien and hostile section than in their own? Perish a thought so blasphemous!

CHAPTER EIGHT
☆ ☆ ☆ ☆

How few of us, too, have ever analyzed the famous Emancipation Proclamation; have ever tried to ascertain the proportions of politics, diplomacy, and philanthropy couched therein; have ever regarded its true purport and bearings. Did it free, or seek to free, all the slaves in the land? Oh, no! Only a part. What part? Those in the hands of Lincoln's enemies. Those within the Union lines, those in the hands of friends, were not affected by the proclamation. They remained in bondage so far as this instrument was concerned. Lincoln had been dead nearly a year before total abolition was legally brought about. Outside of the punitive intent, the prime motive of the proclamation was, first, to buttress the Republican Party against the rising tide of Democracy; second, the Union arms against those of the Confederacy. The military end sought was to weaken his enemies by destroying their property. Naturally, he struck at their chief asset – their slaves. If he had been able thereby to destroy any or all of other kinds of their property he would have done so. If his simple mandate would have cut the throat of every work animal, milch cow, fired every roof-tree, and imperiled the honor of every woman in the South, there is no reason to believe that he would have withheld its utterance; for it was his word that sent hundreds of thousands through the South to do these very things.

If we must accept subjugation, even of mind and of spirit; if we must view the whole bloody drama through the eyes of our enemies; if we must believe that the blow came from above and not below; that we not only richly deserved, but sadly needed just what we got – then the right men to honor are the pioneer Abolitionists, Garrison, Wendell Phillips. Gerrit Smith, and men of that feather. They boldly stood for abolition, when to stand meant hatred, contempt, and imminent peril of life and limb. These men had no ulterior motives. They breasted the tide of fortune. Lincoln floated upon it. If we must honor the sowers of the wind whose fearful whirlwind we had to reap, let's honor these, the real heroes of the cataclysm. True, they sent John Brown with pikes to butcher us; but they were perfectly willing to be butchered themselves in the same cause.

No one would deny that Lincoln was an enemy of slavery. He was a product of a class and of an environment that drew in hatred of slavery and of slave-holders with every breath. Moreover, most thinking people, North and South, were enemies of slavery in theory. With Lincoln and the North it was only a theory. With the South it was a fact, a grim fact which, foisted upon us by English and later by Northern greed, time had now riveted upon us. The growth was cancerous. But would you go to your butcher to remove even a cancer?

Emancipation at the time, and in the manner in which Lincoln sought to enforce it, was a politico-military measure, and nothing else. 1862 was election year. Lincoln, great man and statesman as he undoubtedly was, was also politician to the core. And when did your politician, big or little, ever fail to trim his sails to the wind – to save the party and then let the party save everything else? Federal arms had sustained such repeated and disastrous defeats that Northern opinion was turning to the Democratic Party, which favored peace. Defeat stared Republicanism in the face. Something must be done to stem the tide. The Emancipation Proclamation was the answer. While primarily a political move, great things were also expected of it in a military way. It was largely believed that the slaves would rise and deal with Southern women in a way that would cause the Southern armies to crumble in a day, as each man rushed home to save his own.

As a military measure it was the fiasco of the ages. Not a slave stirred or lifted hand. But its political effect was immense. It instantly brought into the Republican camp every cohort of Abolitionism, and held all in line to the end, though these lines bent fearfully under Jackson's blows at Chancellorsville, and again, when soon after the grey columns surged northward to Gettysburg, and even when, much later still, Grant's army recoiled in temporary paralysis from the futile assaults on Lee in the Wilderness.

Still, this is not an attack on Lincoln, nor do I seek to revive sectionalism, further than consistency and self-respect demand. I am well aware that patriotism is a matter of geography. That all depends upon the side of the line on which you were born. But so, also, is renegadism. High moral law demands that we be true to our fellows, our surroundings. The Washingtons and Lees obeyed it. The Arnolds and Iscariots defied it. This is simply an earnest protest against accepting as a Southern hero, a Southern exemplar, a man, no matter how worthy personally, who was a leader of Northernism, and of Northernism in its attitude of implacable hostility to the South and Southern ideals. It is natural that the Negro should honor Lincoln. He gave the Negro freedom. And the North: he gave the North dominion over the South. He carried out Northern ideals of centralism, imperialism. The Southern ideal – State rights, home rule, the palladium the world over of the weak – met destruction at his hands. With glaring inconsistency, we still hold the ideal to be true, while paying homage to the chief instrument of its destruction.

CHAPTER NINE

☆ ☆ ☆ ☆

"Suppose the South had won? What then?" is the common query, usually in tones of utter deprecation. I would reply that the South lost; what then? The blackest page in the annals of our race! Would the Lees, the Davises, the Hamptons, the Vances, the Grahams, the Ashes, the Grimeses, the Clarks, the Jarvises, the Hills, the Carrs, the Ransoms, the Averys, have been less fit to deal with even the tremendous issues left by war than the Sewards, the Wades, the Stevenses, the Holdens, the Tourgees, the Deweeses, the Cuffees, who fumbled them till, with an effort that paralyzed all other endeavors for a generation, we wrenched the helm from their hand?

The War of 1861, notwithstanding the unfortunate slavery complication, was as much a war of liberty as that of 1775, or that of 1642 in the Mother country. It was a struggle for local self-government against centralism and all the evils that have skulked in its shadow – monopoly, trusts, extortion in its protean guises. A quicker exploitation of our resources – and a quicker destruction – has undoubtedly ensued. But where has the wealth gone? Would not those resources be safer in the hands of nature than in the hands that now hold and use them as a lever to oppress and extort?

The war, waged for State rights, for local self-government, the principle for which the flower of our manhood laid down their lives, was the half-conscious effort of our branch of the race – the branch that events have proven to have had the keenest political instincts of all – to avert this torrent of evils; some then plainly disclosed to our clear vision, some even now just emerging from the haze of the days to be.

Then circumstances and heredity had made the South the citadel of conservatism. What a brake on the wild wheels of this mad world her conservatism must have been, could it only have won the prestige of success, had it only been its luck to be backed by the stronger battalions or heavier guns! In all human probability it would have saved us from many of the evils above indicated, as well as the maze of fads, follies, and isms in which we now grope in such utter bewilderment. Even Southern writers have to stultify themselves every time they approach the subject as to what might have been if the victory had been accorded to us instead of our foes.

Loud in praise of the statesmanship of the old South, strong in the belief of the justice of her cause; yet no sooner do they reach the point where the stronger battalions of the North prevail than they drop on their knees and thank Heaven for having saved the South from herself. They thank Providence that instead of giving the South a respite from Northern incendiarism, instead of smoothing her way so that she might put by slavery in the least harmful manner, it brought down upon her three million of armed men, who, destroying the flower of her manhood, breaking the heart of her womanhood, consigning her children to poverty and ignorance, reducing her people to virtual beggars, and would have forced miscegenation, mongrelism, upon her, but for the mettle of her stock! Others may think as they will, but I cannot bring myself to hold any such slanderous opinions of Providence. I cannot see the hand of Providence (though I might a sootier one) in such fell work as, on the one hand suffering Northern Abolition incendiarism to arouse and inflame the resentment of the South, and, on the other hand, Northern ingenuity to invent the cotton gin, thus at the critical moment infinitely increasing the value of slaves, and forestalling the South in her earnest endeavors to put an end to slavery. That the South was denied the inestimable privilege of abolishing this curse which the cruel hand of Fate had fastened upon her, thus saving herself the unspeakable loss and woe and humiliation that the war entailed, is no proof that the Southern way was the wrong way. Success is no proof of right, nor failure of wrong. Yet men whose very religion is founded on faith in One who from the low viewpoint of material things sounded the abysmal depths of failure, now cry aloud that it is. The vessel of iron will ever smash the one of gold against which in the rough mischances of the world it is thrown, though the latter, from the fineness of its material and the nobleness of its design, might be fit to edify mankind forever.

O. W. Blackball.
Kitteell, N. C., January, 1915.

(In regard to race segregation, I would add that the question was extensively discussed at the North in the early part of the war, and Florida suggested as the State to be thus utilized when the South should be subjugated. This being considered too small, Texas was proposed.)

APPENDIX ONE

☆ ☆ ☆ ☆

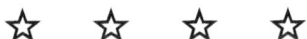

Lincoln and Democracy[2]
by Paul S. Whitcomb,
of Gladstone, Oregon

Nothing so intrigues the mind of the people of the Northern States of the American Republic as the personality of Abraham Lincoln and the imperial American Union. For sixty-two years the crescendo of laudation of Lincoln has been steadily rising, and the end is not yet. For Lincoln was the central figure and the dominating personality in one of the greatest wars of history and, in spite of all the theories of democracy, nothing so appeals to the emotions of men, which are the well

---

1. This article was first published in *Tyler's Quarterly Magazine* for July, 1927, The force of this article is increased by the fact that the writer is of Vermont stock and professes entire change in his opinions as formerly entertained.

springs of eulogy, as martial and imperial glory. People are not given to repudiating the wars they wage or those who lead them into war. Lincoln, himself, was retired from Congress for eight years because of his opposition to the Mexican War.

It is an interesting question as to what Lincoln's place in history would have been if there had been no Civil War with its lurid glow to silhouette his eccentric personality for future generations. At the time of his election to the Presidency he was scarcely more than a local character. He had served in Congress without rising above mediocrity. He had played fast and loose with the questions of slavery and secession without contributing anything original or constructive to the discussion, and what he said only served to further agitate the South and to so compromise his own public position as to make secession inevitable when the Black Republicans came into power.

He has been called a great thinker but his attitude toward both slavery and secession was at once doctrinaire and the result of mechanistic logic which failed to recognize the distinction between the laws of physical science and the laws of human action. With regard to the slaves he appealed from their legal status to the "higher" law, but with regard to secession and the rights of the free and highly civilized white people of the South he argued their rights on the basis of those maxims of despotism which were invented for the express purpose of denying to the people their rightful liberties. He argued that the principles of the Declaration of Independence applied to the Negro but denied that they applied to the free white inhabitants of the States in whose favor they were originally promulgated. He failed to discern that the independence of the slave and the independence of the States involved the same fundamental principle, that the right of secession was absolute and unqualified and no more required oppressive acts to justify it than did the right of the slave to secede from his master. He failed to see that those same class of arguments which denied freedom to the South also denied freedom to all men "and undermined the very foundation of free society."

The indiscriminate and uncritical eulogies which have been heaped upon Lincoln have been pronounced in the face of all but the most superficial facts and as though all the rest of the world was composed of brutes, knaves and fools. There is no evidence that Lincoln was any more honest, kind, accommodating or sagacious than the ordinary run of men. His waging of the Civil War was the very antithesis of common sense and statesmanship. There was no catastrophe potential in secession that in any way justified the waging of the war, viewed simply as a matter of State policy, without reference to the moral and human aspect of the war. It was one of the most colossal bankruptcies of common sense and humane statesmanship known to modern history. As the situation stood in 1860, it were better for the North and the South both that they should separate. The prosperity which followed in the wake of the Civil War was not due to keeping the South in the Union, but to the development of the West. But even if it was, it is a Prussian, and not an American, doctrine that war is a legitimate agent of national progress, that the end justifies the means. We have no right to do evil that good may abound.

Lincoln has been acclaimed the great democrat, yet the greatest act of his career was the very antithesis of democracy. Washington was infinitely a greater statesman and a greater democrat. Robert E. Lee was greater in all around character. It has been too readily assumed that lowliness of birth is evidence of greater democracy. But the man of lowly birth can be no more than a democrat and it is no particular credit to him that he is. But the man of aristocratic birth, who has the privilege and opportunity of being more than a democrat, and yet who remains one, not only in simulation but at heart, can truly claim the title of being a great democrat. The purpose of democracy is not to drag the few down but to lift the many up. It is not to make all common but to make all aristocrats, to diffuse the benefits of culture and good breeding throughout the community. And Washington, who was an aristocrat by birth, because of the largeness of his heart and the breadth of his character became the first democrat through choice and affection. Never can it be truthfully charged against the man who subordinated the military to the civil through seven long miserable, heartbreaking years of revolutionary struggle and at the finish scornfully spurned a crown, that he was lacking in all the great qualities of a democrat.

When Lincoln said that the question of union or disunion could only be settled by war, and ridiculed those who decried force as a legitimate and lawful means of maintaining the Union, arguing that "their idea of means to preserve the object of their great affection would seem to be exceedingly thin and airy," and compared them to free lovers, Washington said, "Let us erect a standard to which the wise and the just can repair, – the result is in the hands of God"; and of the accomplished Union he said that it was "the offspring of our own choice, uninfluenced and unawed, adopted upon full investigation and mature deliberation, completely free in its principles." Washington based the Union upon the democratic principle of free consent. Lincoln ridiculed the basis of democracy, spoke of it as exceedingly thin and airy, likened it to a free love arrangement and asserted that force was the only sound basis of government. He appealed from the basis of democracy to the basis of despotism, from the ballot to the bullet. The Civil War was the result of the putting the new wine of democracy into the old skins of despotism.

The responsibility for the Civil War has been laid at the door of the South on the grounds that they fired the first shot against Fort Sumter. But the grounds beg the question and the responsibility for the war must await the determination of the question as to whether or not the South had a right to secede. If South Carolina had a right to secede she had the right to take Fort Sumter. Lincoln's policy in sitting tight and forcing the South to make the first move was identical with that of Bismarck. "Success," Bismarck said, "essentially depends upon the impression which the origination of the war makes upon us and others; it is important that we should be the party attacked."

But the attack of South Carolina upon Fort Sumter was not an attack upon the North in any such a sense as the attack which Bismarck maneuvered an all too willing Napoleon into making upon Prussia. Fort Sumter was historically and geographically an integral part of the soil of South Carolina. It was there, as Lincoln said in his special message to Congress, for the protection of the people of South Carolina. It was an integral and vital part of their system of common defense. It symbolized the right of these people to defend themselves – a right which is basic to all other rights and which is the very test of manhood. Deny a man or a group of men the right to defend themselves and you deny them all other rights, for what a man has not the right to protect it cannot be reasonably and intelligently argued he has a right to at all.

Fundamentally and vitally the fort belonged to the people of South Carolina. The site of the fort had been ceded to the Federal Government for the protection of the City of Charleston, and the moneys with which the fort had been constructed were drawn by taxation from the people of the States by methods to which all the States had agreed in ratifying the Constitution. South Carolina had contributed her share and was morally entitled to a division of the common property. As to the legal phase of it there was none, for there was no law governing the subject, regardless of the fact that no technical, legal grounds can justify such a social catastrophe as war. War defeats the very end of law and government, which is the conservation of human values.

In spite of the persistent attempt, carried on through school histories and by partizan historians in general, to brand the people of the South in general, and of South Carolina in particular, as so many hell-bent hot heads, the fact is that the secession movement was done "decently and in order." They did not wantonly and in undue haste fire upon Fort Sumter. They sent a commission to Washington to negotiate a peaceful settlement of all questions arising from secession. The assertion that secession was an essentially war-like act was a Federal doctrine and not a Southern doctrine. It was not until this commission had been snubbed on the narrow, childish legalism that the people of the South had no right to speak for themselves, that the people of South Carolina took the only other course open to them and asserted their rights by force of arms.

In general principle the right of the people of South Carolina to dispossess the Federal Government of Fort Sumter involves no more than the right of any property owner to discharge a watchman hired to protect his property. The Federal Government had no more reasonable or moral right to wage war against the people of South Carolina and destroy their lives and property than a discharged watchman would have to destroy the property he was hired to protect. The authority of government is not an end in itself but a means to an end. The attempt to give to civil authority a special extra moral status is without ethical or social warrant and is simply one of the superstitions invented by despots as a means of awing the people and maintaining themselves in power.

Unionists would deny that two times two make four if it were necessary to vindicate the Civil War. To them no statement of principle is valid in favor of the independence of the South and against the war. Secession itself is a true principle when exercised in favor of the Union, as Lincoln declared in the case of the secession of the forty-nine counties of Old Virginia.

The issues involved in the Civil War were not of concern solely to the generation which fought the war but are questions of eternal right and wrong, and are subject to the law of Lincoln's doctrine that no question is settled until it is settled right. The objection that the war is water over the dam, and that the problems of the present demand our attention, is valid providing that history is all bunk and that there is nothing to learn from our past. But the problems of the present are largely the legacy of the past, and if the past had settled them right they wouldn't confront us at the present time. It has only been since the late war that an English Premier has quoted the arguments of Lincoln against secession as an answer to the principles of the Declaration of Independence as put forward in defense of the right of the Irish to freedom. And the struggle of Ireland for freedom antedates our Revolutionary War by a century and a half and involved and involves the same questions.

It is thus that our past rises up to meet us and, as Lincoln said of slavery, "deprives our republican example of its just influence in the world." In setting up the sovereignty of the Union as a basis for making war against the seceding States and as a fence against European interference he was acting upon the same principle that if one man chooses to kill another, neither that man nor any third man has a right to object. The logic of the Civil War was that the right to govern is paramount over the right to live, that man is made for government, rather than that government is made for man, and that for men to claim the right of self-government is to deserve and incur the death penalty.

Lincoln's arguments against the right of the South to independence were drawn from baseless exaggerations, the fatalistic sequence of mechanistic logic, an imperial and authoritarian interpretation of the Constitution which ignored its humanitarian purpose, a strange hodge podge of the maxims of monarchical political science, and an instinctive metaphysical attitude toward government.

Lincoln said of slavery that it was the only thing that endangered the perpetuity of this Union and that it was the *sine qua non* of secession, but from the constitutional and historical standpoint this is not true. Slavery, as he admitted, was "indeed older than the Revolution." It existed previous to the Constitution and the Union was formed in spite of it. Both from the standpoint of the Constitution and sound statesmanship it was not slavery but the intemperate fanatical Abolition movement that endangered the Union.

These Abolitionists proposed to apply all the principles of the Declaration of Independence to a race of people that were totally unprepared for self-government.

It was the intemperate, arrogant, self-righteous and academic attitude of the Abolitionists that made any constructive solution of the slavery question impossible and led the six cotton States to withdraw from the Union.

The right to withdraw was early claimed. As a matter of historical fact, South Carolina had threatened to secede over the tariff. The Colonies seceded from Britain over a question of local self-government. Belgium seceded from Holland and Norway from Sweden, where no question of slavery was involved.

Lincoln said of secession that it was the destruction of the country, of the Union, of the nation and of the liberties of the people and of the institutions of the country. He said, "We have, as all will agree, a free government, where every man has a right to be equal with every other man. In this great struggle, this form of government and every form of human right is endangered if our enemies succeed." The argument was absolutely senseless. One would think to read the argument that some Napoleon, Cæsar or Alexander the Great were attempting to conquer the Southern people and set up a despotism and that Lincoln was waging a war in aid and defense of those people, rather than that those people were seeking to do nothing more than govern themselves and that Lincoln was warring to conquer them, to keep them from exercising their rightful liberties.

Secession was not, in any substantial sense,

the destruction of the nation, nor was it in a proper sense the destruction of the Union. A nation is simply a corporation through which men exercise certain of their rights, just as they exercise other of their rights through their other organizations.

Secession did not destroy the nation, but merely altered it. The Union existed when there were only thirteen States composing it, and it would have continued to exist when there were twenty States left with a boundless public domain.

As for the liberties of the people, all their liberties would have remained intact. Furthermore in spite of the gravity of the situation as it existed in 1789, Washington never proposed to use force to compel a Union.

In his Missouri Compromise speech Lincoln said: "I trust I understand and truly estimate the right of self-government. My faith in the proposition that each man should do precisely as he pleases with all which is exclusively his own lies at the foundation of all the sense of justice there is in me. I extend the principle to communities of men as well as to individuals. I so extend it because it is politically wise, as well as naturally just; politically wise in saving us from broils about matters which do not concern us. The doctrine of self-government is right, – absolutely and eternally right."

No argument could give any stronger support to the right of secession than this argument in favor of freedom for the slave. If the inhabitants of the States are men, is it not to that extent a total destruction of self-government to say that they shall not govern themselves? When the people of the North govern themselves that is self-government; but when they govern themselves and also govern the people of the South, that is more than self-government – that is despotism.

The Negro was the beneficiary rather than the victim of slavery, as Booker T. Washington has admitted. Lincoln's talk about "unrequited toil" ignores the fact that the condition of the Negro was better under slavery than it was in Africa; it ignores the fact that as compared to white laborers of equal mentality he was not deprived of any substantial rights; it ignores the economic and social status of Northern so-called "free" labor which bordered closely upon serfdom; and it ignores the contribution of management to production. The strong probability is that the Negro received at least as great a share, in proportion to what he contributed to production, as did the technically free Northern laborer.

In any event civil war was no more a legitimate remedy for slavery than were the reputedly revolutionary methods of the I. W. W. a proper remedy for the wrongs inflicted upon free labor by Northern capitalists.

In his first inaugural address Lincoln said: "I hold that in contemplation of universal law and of the Constitution, the Union of these States is perpetual. Perpetuity is implied, if not expressed, in the fundamental law of all national governments. It is safe to assert that no government proper ever had a provision in its organic law for its own termination. Continue to execute all the express provisions of our National Constitution, and the Union will endure forever – it being impossible to destroy it except by some action not provided for in the instrument itself."

The argument views States simply as political abstractions. It ignores "States" as denoting an organization of men. It assumes that there is some authority capable of making a contract binding upon all generations of men which shall, throughout the course of time, inhabit a certain territory. It assumes that a few hundred thousand voters living along the Atlantic seaboard a century and a half ago possessed authority over all generations of men which may throughout the course of time inhabit all the country from the

Atlantic to the Pacific seaboard.

The Southern people of 1860 had never entered into "a clear compact of government." It is true that a generation of men previously inhabiting the same territory had done so, but that was not their affair. One generation possesses no such authority over future generations. Political theorists may call this anarchy, but they take their theories too seriously. Men do not maintain government because their granddaddy said they should any more than they live in houses, or eat three square meals a day, or go to church because their granddaddy said they should. In some notes on government Lincoln said: "Most governments have been based, practically, on the denial of the equal rights of men, as I have, in part stated them; ours began by affirming those rights."

In asserting that if we continue to execute all the express provisions of the Constitution the Union will last forever, Lincoln asserted no more than is true of any institution whose charter runs in perpetuity. But the assertion contains no argument against secession. Theorize, as men will, with regard to the basis of government it must conform to rational and moral reasoning, and there is no rational and moral reasoning to support the assumption that one generation can bind another generation in any such a way as is implicit in Lincoln's interpretation of the idea of perpetuity as applied to the Union.

Lincoln neglected to draw the distinction between the right to dissolve an organization and the right to withdraw or secede from it. The one is a right which belongs to the members as a whole while the other is a right inherent if not expressed in the laws of any organization, except as membership therein partakes of the nature of a contractual obligation involving a consideration. But the Union is not of such a nature and there is no authority by which such a perpetual obligation could be established.

In arguing that secession was the essence of disintegration and anarchy Lincoln asked, "why may not any portion of a new confederacy" – arbitrarily secede again – "Is there such perfect identity of interests among the States to compose a new union, as to produce harmony only, and prevent renewed secession? Plainly, the central idea of secession is the essence of anarchy. A majority, held in restraint by constitutional checks and limitations, is the only true sovereign of a free people."

Grant has admitted in his *Memoirs* that if the Southern States had been allowed to secede, they would have set up a government that would have been real and respected, and the assertion that secession was the essence of anarchy was purely academic. The essence of secession is not anarchy but freedom, independence and nationalism.

Lincoln asserted that, "All who cherish disunion sentiments are now being educated to the exact temper of doing this [continuous disintegration]." He could have better argued that all who cherish warlike sentiments are being educated to the temper of conquest. His argument that secession was the essence of anarchy and that the movement could end only in the complete disintegration of society is answered by his own words that, "Happily the human mind is not so constituted."

But while the central idea of secession is not the essence of anarchy, war is anarchy. "It is the essence of war to summon force to decide questions of justice – a task for which it has no pertinence."

After being brought up to the idea that the Southern leaders were so many hasty hotheads, it is disconcerting to read in the speeches of their real leaders the fairness, calmness and friendliness with which they faced the situation. And this attitude was not only in their speeches, but in their actions as well. They took only those measures which any people who had determined upon their course, would have taken as a matter of good judgment and precaution.

Lincoln asked, "Why should there not be a patient confidence in the ultimate justice of the people?" and again, "Will you hazard so desperate a step while there is any possibility that any portion of the ills you fly from have no real existence?" He had better have asked why he should not have a patient confidence in the ultimate justice of the Southern people and why he should hazard so desperate a step as war while there was any possibility that the evils of secession had no real existence. He had said of the Southern people that in point of justice he did not consider them inferior to any people and that devotion to the Constitution was equally great on both sides.

The South in seceding did not take anything that by any moral principle belonged to the North, and if the Civil War is to be justified, either upon policy or principle, it must be upon a showing that secession was an invasion of the rights of the people of the North that justified the taking of human life. No abstract, highly synthetic and controversial theories of sovereignty can justify the taking of human life. Man acting gregariously possesses no other right to take life than is possessed by the individual. Murder is murder, whether it is committed by one man or twenty millions of men, and the empiricisms of political so called "science" constitute no authority for murder. The idea that a "nation" can commit murder in order to achieve a fancied destiny is the essence of immorality and imperialism.

Lincoln said, "This country, with its institutions belongs to the people who inhabit it. Whenever they shall grow weary of the existing government, they can exercise their constitutional right of amending it, or their revolutionary right to dismember or overthrow it." His theory was that the territory of the United States belonged to the people as a whole as sovereign proprietor. That the soil of South Carolina did not belong to the people of South Carolina, who inhabit it, but to the people of the United States as a whole.

The theory is a legacy from feudalism and monarchy and as applied to a republican Union or State is the essence of communism. Democracy is an association of equals.

Under monarchy or feudalism the title to both person and property ultimately resided in the monarch or lord. It was this principle which was the cause of the War of 1812 when England asserted that once a subject always a subject, just as Lincoln claimed that once a State in the Union always a State in the Union.

The right of expatriation, which is simply

a right of personal secession, is an acknowledged American right and has been ever since Jefferson directed the affairs of the nation. We fought for it in the War of 1812 and incorporated it in the Burlingame treaty with China. This right is absolutely inconsistent with the description of the Southern peoples as rebels and traitors and the calling of them to return to their "allegiance" to the Federal Government. The idea of "allegiance" is that of the relation of an inferior to a superior and not of the citizens of a republic to their republican society.

Certainly there is a territorial consideration in the formation of civil society, but that consideration is born of practical necessity and must end with the necessity. But no such consideration was involved in the secession of the Southern States. They were as able to govern themselves as were the people of the North or of England or of France or any other State. There are however no constitutional grounds for the pretense of territorial sovereignty on the part of the United States Government. The Government of the United States is simply the joint and common agent of the States, members of the Union, just as a farmers cooperative is the agent of its members. The basic principles involved in the Union of States are the same as those involved in the agricultural co-operatives. And as I have previously observed, the United States cannot, under the Constitution, exercise exclusive legislative jurisdiction over the site for its own capitol, or the sites for forts, dockyards or other needful public buildings without first getting the consent of the legislature in which the site is situated. To call such a government a territorial sovereign is absurd.

The people of South Carolina possess exactly the same natural, moral and fundamental rights as against the people of the State of New York that the people of Canada do.

Lincoln spoke of the people as possessing a revolutionary right, but such talk is to deny their sovereignty and imply the sovereignty of the Constitution. Revolution is the overthrow of the sovereign, not of the Constitution or of the Government. The people do not derive their sovereign authority from the Constitution. It is not the Constitution of the people but of the Federal Government and is also the record of a compact between the States.

Lincoln admitted that the Government could be overthrown and the Union dismembered. A successful rebel becomes a revolutionist and his success vindicates his rebellion. It is a curious doctrine that success vindicates what would otherwise be a crime.

As a matter of historical fact these rebellions were generally efforts on the part of the people to regain their rightful liberties. As to whether or not secession was revolution depends upon whether the people of the seceding States possessed the right to run their own business.

Lincoln said of secession that, "It recognizes no fidelity to the Constitution, no obligation to maintain the Union," but the fact is, there is no obligation on the part of the States to maintain the Union. He said, "Surely each man has as strong a motive now to preserve our liberties as each had then to establish them;" but in order to justify war he must have a stronger motive, for the Union wasn't established by force and the war overthrew those very liberties for which the Revolutionary War was fought and the Union created – the right of each State to govern itself. He said, "This Union shall never be abandoned, unless the possibility of its existence shall cease to exist without the necessity of throwing passengers and cargo overboard." A more accurate analogy would be to compare the Union to a fleet of ships sailing in voluntary convoy for mutual protection and Lincoln's act in waging war to the act of the elected commander of such a convoy in sinking any ship that seceded from the convoy.

Of the States Lincoln said they "have their status in the Union, and they have no other legal status. If they break from this, they can do so only against law and by revolution. The Union, and not themselves separately, procured their independence and their liberty. The Union is older than any of the States and, in fact, it created them as States. Originally some dependent colonies made the Union, and, in turn, the Union threw off their old dependence for them, and made them States, such as they are."

Lincoln here pretends to be arguing upon legal grounds. The force of his argument lies in the implication that the Union had the legal authority to create those "dependent colonies, States, such as they are." But the union of which he speaks possessed no legal status or authority whatever. It was purely an illegal, revolutionary union whose acts depended for their force upon ratification by the respective colonies represented in the Continental Congress or tacit consent. It was ridiculous for Lincoln to impute legality to such a union while denying it to the Confederacy which was established upon the same legal authority as was the United States.

Lincoln hypostatizes the Union and speaks of it achieving the independence of the

States. But the Union was not a personality or an entity but simply a condition of co-operation.

Water cannot rise higher than its source; derived power cannot be superior to the power from which it is derived and the Federal Union cannot be superior to the States that created it. The Constitution is supreme only in the sense that the laws of any organization are supreme over its members, so long as they remain members.

Contrary to Webster's assertion and the language of the enacting clause of the Constitution, it was not ratified either by the authority of the people of the United States or directly by the people of the States.

The phrase, "people of the United States," does not bear out the argument of Webster and the imperialists, that the people of the United States are united. The phrase is not "united people" but "united States." The present Constitution was ratified when the Union was still based upon the Articles of Confederation. The mode of ratification ignored the Articles entirely and referred back to the prime authority of the State legislature.[3]

---

3. This is an inaccurate statement if Whitcomb referred to the authority possessed by the State legislatures rather than that which stood behind them. The legislatures were but secondary authorities; the prime authority, or sovereignty, resided with

It is only in a subjective or administrative sense that the people of the United States constitute one people. In the exercise of their sovereign powers they do, and always have resolved themselves into sovereign States. Marshall argued that the United States was sovereign to the extent of its authority, but it is no more sovereign than any agent is sovereign. Its powers are delegated powers. In waging the Revolutionary War the men of 1776 were fighting for everything that Webster and Lincoln argued against. The men of 1776 denied the rightfulness of the asserted British sovereignty. They asserted that they were men with all the rights of men, and Englishmen with all the constitutional rights of Englishmen, and that their colonial situation had no political significance, that it was not a crime for which they could be punished by depriving them of their rights of self-government.

They claimed for their colonial legislature a constitutional parity with Parliament, possessed of exclusive legislative jurisdiction within its respective colony and that the Empire was bound simply by the theoretical sovereignty of

---

the body politic – the people of the several States. Whereas the Articles of Confederation were established by the State legislatures, the Constitution was ratified by the people themselves, acting through their own delegates in convention assembled.

the crown. They did not fight for union, but for the right of each colony to complete self-government.

The question as to whether the Union is a league, confederation, federation or nation, is not a vital one but is purely technical and is simply a matter of the mode of administration, of the extent of organization, not of obligation. Because it employs some machinery of government also used in national organizations is no more reason for calling it a "nation" than there would be for calling a gasoline engine a steam engine because of certain features they possess in common.

The assertion that secession is treason is not borne out by the nature of the Union, by the constitutional definition of treason or the nature of treason itself, or by the principles of democracy. Treason is a crime against the "sovereign." The Union is an association of co-equal States and the Federal Government is simply the common agent of those States. The Constitution says that "Treason against the United States shall consist in levying war against them, or in adhering to their enemies," etc. It uses the plural "them" and "their" denoting an association of sovereigns rather than a unitary sovereign. It was Lincoln who committed treason and not the States. Lincoln overthrew eleven sovereign States and State governments, which even according to Webster were the equal of the Federal Government. The idea of the sovereignty of the whole people of the United States is purely an imperialistic dogma. Analyzed, it means that the people of Oregon are sovereign over the people of South Carolina and that the people of South Carolina are sovereign over the people of Oregon. The people of Oregon possess no more sovereign rights in the government of the people of South Carolina than they do in the government of the people of Canada or Mexico. The doctrine is indefensible by the principles of democracy.

Lincoln has been put forward as the great exemplar of Christianity, but the Civil War was fought in diametrical opposition not only to every principle of democracy, but of Christianity. What he said of John Brown may also be said of Lincoln that, "It could avail himself nothing that he might think himself right." That cannot excuse violence, bloodshed and treason.

Like the enthusiast, of whom Lincoln said that he "broods over the oppression of a people till he fancies himself commissioned by Heaven to liberate them," so Lincoln brooded until he fancied himself commissioned by Heaven as a modern Moses raised up to lead the "oppressed" slaves to freedom, and when the war had brought such misery and destruction that it could no longer be justified upon the original object of saving the Union he then attributed to it the added character of a divinely appointed means of punishing the North and the South for "the bondsman's two hundred and fifty years of unrequited toil."

But, regardless of the fact that slavery was in no sense a unique crime, Christ said that He "came, not to judge the world, but that the world through Him might be saved." The Civil War was a greater crime than slavery. Both were a denial of the right of self-government, but where slavery simply took away the unrestrained barbaric freedom of the Negro and put him to constructive employment, the war destroyed the very lives of those who had been previously denied the right of self-government. Lord Morley has said that it is not enough that we should do good. We must do it in the right way. War was no more a righteous method of perpetuating the Union than it would have been a righteous method of originally forming the Union. It was no more a righteous method of keeping the Southern States inside the Union than it would be a righteous method for bringing Canada into the Union or the United States into the League of Nations. The end does not justify the means.

Lincoln would have been a true democrat

if he had perpetuated the Union by the method by which Washington formed it. He would have been a true Christian if he had followed the example of that other Abraham who said to his kinsman, "Let there be no strife, I pray thee, between me and thee – for we be brethren. Is not the whole land before thee? Separate thyself, I pray thee, from me; if thou wilt take the left hand, then I will go to the right, or if thou depart to the right hand, then I will go to the left."

APPENDIX TWO

☆　☆　☆　☆

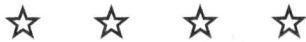

The Fallacies of the Gettysburg Address
by Greg Loren Durand

Four score and seven years ago our fathers brought forth on this continent, a new nation, conceived in Liberty, and dedicated to the proposition that all men are created equal.

Now we are engaged in a great civil war, testing whether that nation, or any nation so conceived and so dedicated, can long endure. We are met on a great battlefield of that war. We have come to dedicate a portion of that field, as a final resting place for those who here gave their lives that that nation might live. It is altogether fitting and proper that we should do this.

But in a larger sense, we can not dedicate – we can not consecrate – we can not hallow – this ground. The brave men, living and dead, who struggled here, have consecrated it, far above our poor power to add or detract. The world will little note, nor long remember what we say here, but it can never forget what they did here. It is for us the living, rather, to be dedicated here to the unfinished work which they who fought here have thus far so nobly advanced. It is rather for us to be here dedicated to the great task remaining before us – that from these honored dead we take increased devotion to that cause for which they gave the last full measure of devotion – that we here highly resolve that these dead shall not have died in vain – that this nation, under God, shall have a new birth of freedom – and that government of the people, by the people, for the people, shall not perish from the earth.

In the words of H.L. Mencken, "The Gettysburg speech was at once the shortest and the most famous oration in American history. . . . It is genuinely stupendous. But let us not forget that it is poetry, not logic; beauty, not sense."[1] Abraham Lincoln's Gettysburg Address is certainly one of the best examples of propaganda to ever have been foisted upon the American people. That it has survived for so long in popular opinion as a speech of great statesmanship aptly demonstrates the power which words, however

---

1. *Five Men at Random* (1922), pages 171, 176.

speciously strung together, have to affect the emotions and minds of those who hear them.

However, the Address, when delivered on 19 November 1863, did not garner the admiration from its original audience that it does in our day. In fact, there is ample evidence to suggest that the now-familiar words were not all spoken on that day in Pennsylvania. Ward Lamon, a close companion of Lincoln during his years as President, who sat beside him on the platform, testified that the received text "is not the speech Mr. Lincoln made at Gettysburg. . . . I state it as a fact and without fear of contradiction, that this Gettysburg speech was not regarded as a production of extraordinary merit, nor was it commented on as such until after the death of Mr. Lincoln." He then recalled Lincoln's words to him after he had resumed his seat: "Lamon, that speech was like a wet blanket on the audience. I am distressed about it."[2] John Nicolay, who was Lincoln's personal secretary during the war, also said the speech was revised after the President had returned to Washington.[3]

Henry E. Shephard of Baltimore said:

It is now quite well known that Mr. Lin-

---

2. *Recollections of Abraham Lincoln* [1895], p. 173
3. *Century Magazine,* February, 1894

coln did not write the Gettysburg speech as it appears in all text books on American Literature which have been written by Northern men, and in nearly all readers used in Southern schools. His intimate friend Lamon's testimony is corroborated by William Seward, Edward Everett, who sat on the stage with him, and others who were present when the speech was made. And yet Jefferson Davis, the author of several published books, is omitted from the text books of American Literature written by Northern men, and Abraham Lincoln put in because of a speech he never wrote.[4]

Finally, W.H. Cunningham, a reporter for the Montgomery (Missouri) *Star* who was present at the dedication of the Gettysburg National Cemetery, likewise stated:

It was my privilege to be present at the dedication of the Soldiers National Cemetery at Gettysburg the afternoon of November 19, 1863, and to hear the now famous address of Abraham Lincoln on that occasion. I can bear witness to the fact that this address, pronounced by Edward Everett to be unequaled in the annals of oratory, fell upon unappreciative ears, was entirely unnoticed and wholly disap-

---

4. Quoted by Mildred Lewis Rutherford, *Truths of History* (1920), p. 121

pointing to a majority of the hearers. This may have been owing in part to the careless and undemonstrative delivery of the orator, but the fact is that he had concluded his address and resumed his seat before most of the audience realized that he had begun to speak. It was my good fortune as a newspaper correspondent to occupy a place directly beside Mr. Lincoln when he delivered this brief oration. . . .

At the conclusion of Mr. Everett's scholarly oration, Mr. Lincoln faced the vast audience. He looked haggard and pale and wore a shabby overcoat, from an inside pocket of which he drew a small roll of manuscript. He read his address in a sort of drawling monotone, the audience remaining silent. The few pages were soon finished. Mr. Lincoln doubled up his manuscript, thrust it back into his overcoat pocket and sat down – not a word, not a cheer, not a shout. The people looked at one another, seeming to say, "Is that all?"

I am well aware that accounts have differed as to the manner of this address and its reception by the audience. I was an eyewitness and hearer and my position was immediately beside the speaker, therefore the foregoing account may be relied upon.[5]

---

5. *Blue and Gray: The Patriotic American Magazine* (1894), Volume II, pages 23-24.

Let us assume, for the sake of argument, that the Gettysburg Address was delivered by Lincoln in the same form as it has been passed down through the generations to us. It is noteworthy that in his first Inaugural Address, he had referred twenty times to the United States as "the Union"; not once did he refer to them as a nation. In sharp contrast to this, the word "nation" completely supplanted "union" in the Gettysburg Address, appearing five times. Northern Democrats were calling for a restoration of "the Union as it was," but by 1863, Lincoln had abandoned any pretense of restoring such a Union. As admitted recently by a Columbia law professor, the Address served as the preamble of a new constitution for a completely new nation, which had been conceived thirty years before in the minds of a deceptive Massachusetts Senator (Daniel Webster) and a renegade Supreme Court Justice (Joseph Story), and finally birthed in the usurpations of the sixteenth President in 1861: "The republic created in 1789 is long gone. It died with 600,000 Americans killed in the Civil War. That conflict decided once and forever that the People and the States do not have the power to govern their local lives apart from the nation as a whole."[6]

------

6. George P. Fletcher, "Unsound Constitution," *The New Republic*, June 1997

Lincoln attempted to trace the founding of this fictitious nation back to 1776 – the date of the signing of the Declaration of Independence. Of course, even a cursory reading of that document will expose the fallacy of this assertion. Rather than the indivisible nation envisioned by Lincoln, what we find in the Declaration are thirteen former British colonies *separately* announcing themselves to the world as "free and independent States." There was not even a political Union between those original States until the ratification of the Articles of Confederation five years later. Even then, the States jealously retained their "sovereignty, freedom, and independence" (Article II). This essential sovereignty of the States was again secured in the Tenth Amendment to the Constitution, which states: "The powers not delegated to the United States by the Constitution, nor prohibited by it to the States, are reserved to the States respectively, or to the people."

Lincoln went on in his Address to say that "a great civil war" was being fought by the North to test "whether that nation . . . can long endure," and he memorialized the dead "who here gave their lives that that nation might live" and that "government of the people, by the people, and for the people shall not perish from the earth." With these poetic words, he was in reality memorializing the men in gray, not the men in blue. It was actually the Confederates who were fighting to preserve "government of the people, etc." – the people who comprised the States of the South who had, in their sovereign capacity, entered the Union in order to "secure the blessings of Liberty" to themselves and their posterity. Again exercising this sovereignty, the Southern States withdrew from the Union when their peace and security was threatened by Northern fanatics, who openly proclaimed their contempt for both Constitution and Union. Below are but a few examples of the treasonous rhetoric of such men:

> The Union is a lie. The American Union is an imposture, and a covenant with death, and an agreement with hell. . . . I am for its over-throw. . . . Up with the flag of disunion, that we may have a free and glorious Union of our own.[7]

> How dare any man pray for the return of that festering wrong – that sin and shame – the Union as it was? It is like breaking the tables of the Eternal Law, and dashing them in the face of Jehovah![8]

---

7. William Lloyd Garrison; in Stephen D. Carpenter, *The Logic of History* (1864), p. 56

8. Boston *Commonwealth*; in Carpenter, *ibid.*, p. 118

Lincoln had feigned to distance himself from such revolutionaries, but the fact remains that men of this stripe were to be found in prominent positions in both Congress and in his own Cabinet. These were the men who pulled the strings of their presidential puppet, and Lincoln did not possess the moral fortitude to stand against their radical agenda, as would his successor, Andrew Johnson, during Reconstruction. Contrary to his claim that, should the South win the war, freedom and republican government would "perish from the earth," those lofty ideals were instead buried in the grave of Southern independence by Northern aggression. The defeat of the South in 1865 destroyed – perhaps forever – the liberty which the patriots of 1776 paid for with their own blood.